Working Dogs

by Jessica Quilty

Scott Foresman
is an imprint of

Glenview, Illinois • Boston, Massachusetts • Chandler, Arizona
Upper Saddle River, New Jersey

Photographs

Every effort has been made to secure permission and provide appropriate credit for photographic material. The publisher deeply regrets any omission and pledges to correct errors called to its attention in subsequent editions.

Unless otherwise acknowledged, all photographs are the property of Pearson Education, Inc.

Photo locators denoted as follows: Top (T), Center (C), Bottom (B), Left (L), Right (R), Background (Bkgd)

Cover Dogs/Fotolia; **1** Trevor Wood/Alamy Images; **3** Dogs/Fotolia; **4** Digital Vision/ Getty Images; **5** Peter Anderson/©DK Images; **6** cynoclub/Fotolia; **7** david hancock/ Alamy Images; **8** Trevor Wood/Alamy Images.

ISBN 13: 978-0-328-50825-9
ISBN 10:   0-328-50825-X

8 9 10 11 V010 17 16 15 14 13

These two dogs are border collies.
What do they do? They do a lot!
    They help people on farms. Border
collies are smart.

A border collie watches over the flock.

When the farmer gives a sign, the border collie knows what to do. It brings in the sheep. The dog runs and barks and moves the sheep into the pen.

The dog is not scared of other animals. It can take care of geese too. It moves the geese where the farmer wants them to be.

A border collie pup

This puppy was bought by a farmer. Now he will learn how to work with sheep. He will grow up to be a great helper.

Border collies love to work. They also like to run and play. They have a good time. It is probably lots of fun for them on the farm!

Border collies make the farm pleasant and safe.

"Shall we go get the sheep?" asks the farmer.

"Woof!" bark the dogs.